THE PLEASURES OF PEACE
and Other Poems

THE PLEASURES OF PEACE
and Other Poems

KENNETH KOCH

Grove Press, Inc.   New York

Library of Congress Catalog Card Number: 72-82108

Acknowledgments: "Seine" and "Sleeping with Women"
appeared in *Poetry*. Poems in this volume have also
appeared in *Art and Literature, C Magazine, First
Issue, i.e. The Cambridge Review, Locus Solus, Mother,
Paris Review,* and *The Second Coming;* in *Permanently*
(Tiber Press, New York), *Sleeping with Women* (Black
Sparrow Press, Los Angeles), and *Stamped Indelibly*
(Multiples, New York)

Third Printing

Manufactured in the United States of America

DISTRIBUTED BY RANDOM HOUSE, INC., NEW YORK

To Frank O'Hara

CONTENTS

THE PLEASURES OF PEACE
and Other Poems

SLEEPING WITH WOMEN

Caruso: a voice.
Naples: sleeping with women.
Women: sleeping in the dark.
Voices: a music.
Pompeii: a ruin.
Pompeii: sleeping with women.
Men sleeping with women, women sleeping with women,
    sheep sleeping with women, everything sleeping with
    women.
The guard: asking you for a light.
Women: asleep.
Yourself: asleep.
Everything south of Naples: asleep and sleeping with
    them.
Sleeping with women: as in the poems of Pascoli.
Sleeping with women: as in the rain, as in the snow.
Sleeping with women: by starlight, as if we were angels,
    sleeping on the train,
On the starry foam, asleep and sleeping with them—
    sleeping with women.
Mediterranean: a voice.
Mediterranean: a sea. Asleep and sleeping.
Streetcar in Oslo, sleeping with women, Toonerville
    Trolley
In Stockholm asleep and sleeping with them, in Skansen
Alone, alone with women,
The rain sleeping with women, the brain of the dog-eyed
    genius
Alone, sleeping with women, all he has wanted,
The dog-eyed fearless man.
Sleeping with them: as in *The Perils of Pauline*

Asleep with them: as in Tosca
Sleeping with women and causing all that trouble
As in Roumania, as in Yugoslavia
Asleep and sleeping with them
Anti-Semitic, and sleeping with women,
Pro-canary, Rashomon, Shakespeare, tonight, sleeping with
   women
A big guy sleeping with women
A black seacoast's sleeve, asleep with them
And sleeping with women, and sleeping with them
The Greek islands sleeping with women
The muddy sky, asleep and sleeping with them.
Sleeping with women, as in a scholarly design
Sleeping with women, as if green polarity were a line
Into the sea, sleeping with women
As if wolverines, in a street line, as if sheep harbors
Could come alive from sleeping with women, wolverines
Greek islands sleeping with women, Nassos, Naxos, Kos,
Asleep with women, Mykonos, miotis,
And myositis, sleeping with women, blue-eyed
Red-eyed, green-eyed, yellow reputed, white-eyed women
Asleep and sleeping with them, blue, sleeping with women
As in love, as at sea, the rabbi, asleep and sleeping with
   them
As if that could be, the stones, the restaurant, asleep and
   sleeping with them,
Sleeping with women, as if they were knee
Arm and thigh asleep and sleeping with them, sleeping
   with women.
And the iris peg of the sea
Sleeping with women
And the diet pill of the tree
Sleeping with women
And the apology the goon the candlelight

The groan: asking you for the night, sleeping with women
Asleep and sleeping with them, the green tree
The iris, the swan: the building with its mouth open
Asleep with women, awake with man,
The sunlight, asleep and sleeping with them, the moving
    gong
The abacus, the crab, asleep and sleeping with them
And moving, and the moving van, in London, asleep with
    women
And intentions, inventions for sleeping with them
Lands sleeping with women, ants sleeping with women,
    Italo-Greek or Anglo-French orchestras
Asleep with women, asleep and sleeping with them,
The foam and the sleet, asleep and sleeping with them,
The schoolboy's poem, the crippled leg
Asleep and sleeping with them, sleeping with women
Sleeping with women, as if you were a purist
Asleep and sleeping with them.
Sleeping with women: there is no known form for the
    future
Of this undreamed-of view: sleeping with a chorus
Of highly tuned women, asleep and sleeping with them.
Bees, sleeping with women
And tourists, sleeping with them
Soap, sleeping with women; beds, sleeping with women
The universe: a choice
The headline: a voice, sleeping with women
At dawn, sleeping with women, asleep and sleeping with
    them.
Sleeping with women: a choice, as of a mule
As of an island, asleep or sleeping with them, as of a
    Russia,
As of an island, as of a drum: a choice of views: asleep
    and sleeping with them, as of high noon, as of a

choice, as of variety, as of the sunlight, red student,
    asleep and sleeping with them,
As with an orchid, as with an oriole, at school, sleeping
    with women, and you are the one
The one sleeping with women, in Mexico, sleeping with
    women
The ghost land, the vectors, sleeping with women
The motel man, the viaduct, the sun
The universe: a question
The moat: a cathexis
What have we done? On Rhodes, man
On Samos, dog
Sleeping with women
In the rain and in the sun
The dog has a red eye, it is November
Asleep and sleeping with them, sleeping with women
This June: a boy
October: sleeping with women
The motto: a sign; the bridge: a definition.
To the goat: destroy; to the rain: be a settee.
O rain of joy: sleeping with women, asleep and sleeping
    with them.
Volcano, Naples, Caruso, asleep and sleeping, asleep and
    sleeping with them
The window, the windrow, the hedgerow, irretrievable
    blue,
Sleeping with women, the haymow, asleep and sleeping
    with them, the canal
Asleep and sleeping with them, the eagle's feather, the
    dock's weather, and the glue:
Sleeping with you; asleep and sleeping with you: sleeping
    with women.
Sleeping with women, charming aspirin, as in the rain, as
    in the snow,

14

Asleep and sleeping with you: as if the crossbow, as of the
    moonlight
Sleeping with women: as if the tractate, as if d'Annunzio
Asleep and sleeping with you, asleep with women
Asleep and sleeping with you, asleep with women, asleep
    and sleeping with you, sleeping with women
As if the sun, as of Venice and the Middle Ages' "true
Renaissance had just barely walked by the yucca
Forest" asleep and sleeping with you
In China, on parade, sleeping with women
And in the sun, asleep and sleeping with you, sleeping
    with women,
Asleep with women, the docks, the alley, and the prude
Sleeping with women, asleep with them.
The dune god: sleeping with women
The dove: asleep and sleeping with them
Dials sleeping with women; cybernetic tiles asleep and
    sleeping with them
Naples: sleeping with women; the short of breath
Asleep and sleeping with you, sleeping with women
As if I were you—moon idealism
Sleeping with women, pieces of stageboard, sleeping with
    women
The silent bus ride, sleeping with you.
The chore: sleeping with women
The force of a disaster: sleeping with you
The organ grinder's daughter: asleep with bitumen, sun-
    shine, sleeping with women,
Sleeping with women: in Greece, in China, in Italy, sleep-
    ing with blue
Red green orange and white women, sleeping with two
Three four and five women, sleeping on the outside
And on the inside of women, a violin, like a vista, women,
    sleeping with women

In the month of May, in June, in July
Sleeping with women, "I watched my life go by" sleeping
with women
A door of pine, a stormfilled valentine asleep and sleeping
with them
"This Sunday heart of mine" profoundly dormoozed with
them
They running and laughing, asleep and sleeping with
them
"This idle heart of mine" insanely "shlamoozed" asleep
and sleeping with them,
They running in laughter
To the nearest time, oh doors of eternity
Oh young women's doors of my own time! sleeping with
women
Asleep and sleeping with them, all Naples asleep and
sleeping with them,
Venice sleeping with women, Burgos sleeping with
women, Lausanne sleeping with women, hail depth-
divers
Sleeping with women, and there is the bonfire of Crete
Catching divorce in its fingers, purple sleeping with
women
And the red lights of dawn, have you ever seen them,
green ports sleeping with women, acrobats and
pawns,
You had not known it ere I told it you asleep with women
The Via Appia Antica asleep with women, asleep and
sleeping with them
All beautiful objects, each ugly object, the intelligent
world,
The arena of the spirits, the dietetic whisky, the storms
Sleeping with women, asleep and sleeping with them,

Sleeping with women. And the churches in Antigua, sleep-
   ing with women
The stone: a vow
The Nereid: a promise—to sleep with women
The cold—a convention: sleeping with women
The carriage: sleeping with women
The time: sometimes
The certainty: now
The soapbox: sleeping with women
The time and again nubile and time, sleeping with
   women, and the time now
Asleep and sleeping with them, asleep and asleep, sleep-
   ing with women, asleep and sleeping with them,
   sleeping with women.

IRRESISTIBLE

Dear miles of love, the Solomon barefoot machine is
  quinting! dial aster, dial aster!
The ornery bench of wet state painters is minnowing into
  the dew! phosphorus seems like music lessons.
O bestiary of whose common childhood wings put the
  dials' acreage jollily into place, kneading
Together the formative impulses of a shirt front. O
  Crimea!
Sweet are the uses of adversity and. Sea lions dash
  through an impulse and. The keynote is yellow
Basement. My suffrage has created this hippopotamus.
  Welcome!
Welcome to the Greek lesson, infinitesimal shelves! art!
  this yowl is Beethoven
Speaking silence orangutan armament flute tea angel.
  What! O clear remains of luck's dial!
Ill men have no energy. Quonset hut! Backgammon inside
  the persimmon garage factory
Of knee length portmanteaux, Canadians! Win, win with
  Doctor Einstein! Once
Coffee laughed in boiling sleeves, Chicago lakefront. O
  pullman trade of keys!
Wednesday Bryn Mawr create the college shirt lesson
  peanut armada. Ah, coo!
Everything matronly impulses. Sophomore we stare at the
  sea. Love is a big bunch of laundry. My eye is a
  radish. In Labor Day
Comedies momentary openings jump oak trees by the by
  grape soda. Goodbye, Beethoven! Net
Whales jump about, decide, decide! The opera house of
  K.K. Clothes

C.C. April does and goes, A. Rainboat wink, ha!

Surely surely surely the sea has suffragettes' nailpolish
kinky kimonos' calcium cogentness! Weights!

The plaza of hirsute wishes has now stumbled into the
waste

Secede paper street arf crossing car canoe boxing frog
liverwurst

Pajamas equalitarianism pool-game sissiness Calderon
Shakespeare. The sea limps!

Copper April wire has dean bazooka quiescent her chair
foot. Haven't you met

Lionel Food? After the archery pond soda left shirt bonita.
We haven't met at the carpet-ball game.

Dials of Nice! your cork fume is showing! thou dazzling
beach! O honest peach Cyrano de Bergerac of golf
pins!

Wednesday my hand, Tuesday my face, Wednesday the
beautiful blue bugle; after all,

Water hasn't nearly concealed its pennies under the
discrete lumberyard

Of calcium grasshoppers, nearer than a railroad train to
pinkest shoes

Airing the youthful humps of there each so a big hatbox
of myself! The siren punch, the match box, and

The kittens! Oysters, believe in the velvet kimono. And
Monday my feet are cookies.

Thursday exams. Saturday silver officers. Friday a bowl of
Queen Anne porridge. Paste me to a bar!

Dear miles of love, the Solomon barefoot machine is
quinting! And faster and faster

The blue rose company believes the white air waves to
be getting farther and farther away from yellow!

When December fig newtons steer through the enraged
    gas station
Of lilacs, bringing the crushed tree of doughnuts a suit-
    able ornament
Of laughing bridgework pliable as a kilt in the muddiness
    of this November
Scene starring from juxtapositioning April languor, oceans
Breathless with the touch of Argentina's lilac mouse beat
    in quicksand
Solitude "we cling to me" and backness, O badness, refuse
    calico
Evidence in a cheese timelessness, on banners of soda,
    amid limits, cliffs,
Indians' real estate, clay, peat archery, glazed quarrels,
    pinks,
Clocks, pelts of cloisters, green gasworks, unlimited
    miracle Irish teens'
Asquith, Gorboduc, and Sensation, opened with the cheers
    of an article of commerce
To a "brandished" and "ill" pasteboard canoe of lumber
Fresher than an orchestra's hateful years of guest walk,
    the dachshund at midnight hung
Beside the green lanterns at Wilted Notch Point; eyes
    climb through the horses and amid the chair beans!
Coffee officers gamble on the lantern painting icicles and
    the pyramid!
The cloister of rafters is too tear-bitten to canoe blue
    Afghan mouse.
Earache, earache! its sunshine is brighter than life
    insurance—
Climates! Lovebirds, rooftops! "I've just brought them in
    from Africa."

The country club brings airplanes for canoes. It is spring.
  Old hairpins scrub strawberries.
Cereal says, "Mazy combs." There are cup birds swim-
  ming beside the mask fleet.
Winter is a normal A.C. pockets. Harvest I'll hymnbook.
  With cocoa-jest.
Cuthbert is racing by Arf Arf Swimmer. She's gentle
  clearing. Arf Arch cupboard amid the clouds.
Tree mussed gossamer Atlantic ouch toupées hearing book
  P.S. castiron pasteboard hearing aid in glove society
  fingers'
Alaska with bounce. "I am a raincoat cupboard of ear-
  aches and glass wainscots amid the dreary garden of
  graves unhumorous, bitten as green"—What winter
Hard to close. Manual training is life in China.
My legs aren't a chair; the silver sandpaper is mumbling
  "Storm! confess!"

WEST WIND

It's the ocean of western steel
Bugles that makes me want to listen
To the parting of the trees
Like intemperate smiles, in a
Storm coat evangelistically ground
Out of spun glass and silver threads
When stars are in my head, and we
Are apart and together, friend of my youth
Whom I've so recently met—a fragment of the universe
In our coats, a believable doubling
Of the fresh currents of doubt and
Thought! a winter climate
Found in the Southern Hemisphere and where
I am who offers you to wear,
And in this storm, along the tooth of the street,
The intemperate climate of this double frame of the
    universe.

WE SAILED THE INDIAN OCEAN FOR A DIME

We sailed the Indian Ocean for a dime
And went into Africa for a penny
Refreshing Argentina
Rewarded us with many silver cars
For our toy train   We went to Kansas City
In the hope of finding quarters there
But instead we sailed the Manila Sea
Old sea pencils without landing quarters
Five dollars drew us to Tangiers
We had saved up enough dimes to purchase the bill
There it lies all crisp and green and light
Take it pick it up in your hands it is mine

We spent the five dollars in Biarritz in seven minutes
But at least we had a good meal and now we set sail
I've heard that Milwaukee is full of dimes and quarters
And that Cincinnati is the place for half dollars
I can see all that silver I can see it and I think I want it
Can see the sunlight lighting those silver faces
In far-off Cincinnati
The slim half dollars lying in the leaves
In the blue autumn weather behind the Conservatory of
    Music
Oh give me the money
That I may ascend into the sky
For I have been on so many boats and trains
While endlessly seeking the summits of my life!

THE YOUNG PARK

Hands picked
On her blossoms.
The young park was sad.

In the meadow the dog sat waiting for a shed.
The daisy flowers bloomed and laughed.
That cockroach's fever was bitter.
He worked in the landau.
Margaret's face became all cloaked with linen
When she saw the young park dying among the green
    trees, and answered
The young men who were always so desperately at her
    side: "You see
What will happen to us if I let you do what you've been
Trying. . . . ? Mrs. Cockroach bowed pleasantly
To the hat bear. The sheep were all ado. "I bite,"
Said the happy cockroach.
In the meadows and in the park a dog sat cloaked in red
    woolen fuzz.
He had on a tennis court jacket.
He smelled like a steamship. His green eyes were red.
"You are all hot and heavy and yellow with crying," Jean
    said.
The bat made their voices ring. The plane spun
Down into yo-yos of dizzying aspirin chaffinch.

In sixteen times at the plate
Young Park had made only one hit.
He dug his feet into the gridiron.
The sky was a white lobster.

Of a perfect strike! Young Park
Relaxed and struck lights from the ax.
He exaggerated among the boats.
His engine was scooting for victory.

"It is the imagination of dance addicts,"
Young Park said with one hand
As he held the door open for the new
Manager of the Hens with the other. "That's decorum!"

Had the young park forgotten how to forgive, was that
    her difficulty?
The men rose up and tried to be forgiven in the park.
Then the wet moss became something you must try to
    forget.
I am afraid it is all over with the young park.

"What do I care? Men tell me I am fooling.
In the summer my foot sticks because it is snowing
The ancient regime of reason and the moss is crumbling
Beneath the penitential feet of frisky dogs. Following
My destiny I should die at the age of seventeen, but how
    can I
Live out this year? The marriage van is grumbling
At my feet its maddened "Try!" O Life! and mine a
    mixture
Of husky trees and the oil from a baddened car. O
    disassembled
Garden walls, mayn't you give your pity to a young park?"

This is how Oswald became famous.
His whole conduct was dissimulated:
He changed his name to Fred Smith

And spent his summers in Young Park
Perfecting boiler engines
In the free laboratory they supplied there.
However the Foundation stipulated
No one named Oswald shall be, by Young Park,
Granted the use of its facilities
Without paying, but be obliged to pay six cents
For each kilowatt hour exacted of the lamps
And bulbs of the Young Park Seed and Tree Grant
    Foundation Free Laboratory Stationary Fund Facili-
    ties Buildings. . . .

In Young Park the coppery city girl felt cold,
So she took all her clothes off except
Her gloves and ran into the water with Mr. Southland.

Above the stones
Young Park spoke to the people in a dead language.
He cautioned them to watch out for sparks
From Oswald's shoes. Then he gave them the baseball
    glove
For which they had been waiting for fifteen years.

"These traffic lamps have colors that would be perfect for
    cigarettes," the young park said.

The automobile club had changed its location again, and
    was now located in the zoo.
At the zoo the automobile club was disregarded, everyone
    stared into the chicken cages.
Then one night the young giraffe became hurt, and the
    Zoo River was dammed up.
A boat came down the Zoo River. Inside the boat was
    Dame Oswald.

That boat came to the dam; Dan Cupid played on his quiver; Dame Oswald was left out at the door of the automobile club.

Dame Oswald fell in love with a bear cub she saw whose cage had been left open; and then she reboarded ship with the bear cub.

The next day the zoo reopened its gates to the physical education inspector. He decreed that Zoo River must be reopened.

Thus the automobile club floated out to sea, and the terrible truth of dust is at ease again.

Oswald's victory in the Paris sweepstakes has just been announced; and there is a rumor that he is coming home again.

A grain of sand floats down to the catchy bottom of summer.

At noon the pelvises walk into the green hospital and speak: "The young park is dead.

Young Park has just been killed in a prize fight. Young Park has been ravaged and destroyed by fire."

But here comes Oswald! What an air he has about him!

He looks as though he's raving mad, and there is Margaret on his arm!

I think they are having a bite of cheese before going into the delicatessen.

Stop them and ask them for the news from over there.

There's that dog in a red jacket!

Oswald is really crazy!

Bicycles, the moon and the stars. The seashore.

Look! he's all dressed up, but his mouth is foaming! Aaaahhhhhhhh!

Quick, let's get away from here! You can borrow my blue
    bicycle.
I'll ride slowly down to sea on my orange-and-red one.
The immense men ride swiftly away on green bicycles,
    because the young park is dead.
"Wait a moment!"

"At night, when everything is yellow and green,
You too can come alive
If you believe in me."

POEM

The thing
To do
Is organize
The sea
So boats will
Automatically float
To their destinations.
Ah, the Greeks
Thought of that!
Well, what if
They
Did? We have no
Gods
Of the winds!
And therefore
Must use
Science!

THREE SHORT POEMS

HEANORUPEATOMOS

Unroll this enrollment.
There, you see—
And now we have done.

And back to another day in the bars of Paris.

AN X-RAY OF UTAH

Valley! my whole head is a valley! valley! valley!

RELIGIOUSLY

There is rain in my heart and a boat in the harbor
Greece submerged in the sea   The blue light on its
    waters
A child wanders in torn clothes crying Vacation!

DOSTOEVSKI'S *THE GAMBLER*

Dostoevski's *The Gambler*
Lay on the table.
I opened to page one:
Neshish stroggen baihoosh.

Mantegna's white sculpture,
The Tail of a Dolphin,
Lay slumbering in Italy;
The sea it was blue.

Don Mozart's *Concerto*
Alexander von Wertheim
The Fifth, for piano
And table legs, bouncers and flute

Was silent, on separate pages.
A painting of bankruptcy spilt through the walls;
Its yellow and gray
Exposed it as a goldfish Juan Gris.

My sailboat has crashed
Against a wall,
My domino is spattered with black
Mud. But where is the hashish of Toledo?

HEARING

Hear the beautiful tinny voices of the trumpets
Beside the rushing sound of the great blue waterfall;
See the guns fire, then hear the leaves drop to the ground;
Lie back in your chair—and now there is the clatter of
    pennies!
The familiar scraping noise of the chair feet on the
    ground,
As if a worm had grown six feet tall! And here is the
    worm,
And hear his softly scraping noise at the forest gate.
In the Bourse the diamonds clink and clank against each
    other,
And the violet airplane speaks to the farmland with its
    buzz
From high in the air, but you hear the slice
Of shears and watch the happy gardener's face whiten
As he hears the final throbs of his failing heart.
All is not stillness—far from it. The tinny
Trumpets renew their song among the eglantine's
Too speciously gracious brilliance, and a hen drops
An egg, with infinite gentleness, into the straw.

Who is this young man with the tremendous French horn
    in the garden
With a lady in lilac bending her head to catch each note
That flows, serene and unbidden, from the silvery throat?
I think they are strangers here. Stones fall in the pool.
She smiles, she is very witty, she bends too far, and now
    we hear
The sound of her lilac dress ripping in the soft summer
    air.

For it is summer! Hear the cool rush of the stream and
the heavy black
Vocalism of leaves in the wind. A note then comes, arises
In the air, it is a glass in which a few warm drops of rain
Make music; there are roars and meows, turkeys and
spaniels
Come running to the great piano, which, covered with
pearls,
Gives extra, clinking sounds to your delighted ears;
And the dogs bark, and there is the little thrilled silence
of snails. . . .
Above all else you hear the daisies being torn apart
By tremendous bumblebees who have come here from
another Department!
"Wisteria tapping the house, so comes your blood. . . ."

Now rain, now this earth streams with water!
Hear the tooting of Triton among the clouds
And on the earth! See the trumpets of heaven floating
toward us
Blaring among the wet masses of citron and vermilion
wings!
They play "Put down the cushion on the chair,
Put down the cushion on the chair, put down
The cushion, put it down, put the cushion down on the
chair,
Ra ta ta. . . ." The young man's French horn is wet, it
makes a different noise,
The girl turns her face toward him and he hears strings
(it is another tear in her dress!).
In the kitchen the sound of raspberries being mashed in
the cream
Reminds you of your childhood and all the fantasies you
had then!

In the highest part of an oak tree is a blue bird
Trilling. A drying friend reads *Orlando Furioso*
Sitting on a beach chair; then you hear awnings being
   stretched out!
A basso sings, and a soprano answers him.
Then there is thunder in a clear blue sky,
And, from the earth, a sigh: "This song is finished."

A POEM OF THE FORTY-EIGHT STATES

1

O Kentucky! my parents were driving
Near blue grass when you became
For me the real contents of a glass
Of water also the first nozzle of a horse
The bakery truck floating down the street
The young baboon woman walking without a brace
Over a fiord

The electric chair steamed lightly, then touched
Me. I drove, upward,
Into the hills of Montana. My pony!
Here you are coming along with your master!
Yet I am your master! You're wearing my sweater.
O pony, my pony!

As in a dream I was waiting to be seventh
To smile at my brothers in the happy state of Idaho
Each and every one of them condemned to the electric
        chair!
What have we done? Is it a crime
To shoe horses? Beside a lemon-yellow stream
There seemed to be compact bassoons,
And I was happy and a crackerjack.

My stovepipe hat! Perhaps you think I am Uncle Sam?
No, I am the State of Pennsylvania. . . .
O hills! I remember writing to a city
So as to be contented with my name
Returning in the mails near the mark "Pennsylvania"!

"Somewhere over that hill is Georgia."
What romance there was for me in the words the old man
said!
I wanted to go, but was afraid to wander very far.
Then he said, "I will take you in my wagon of hay."
And so we rode together into the Peach State.
I will never forget that day, not so long as I live,
I will never forget the first impressions I had in Georgia!

2

In Zanesville, Ohio, they put a pennant up,
And in Waco, Texas, men stamped in the streets,
And the soldiers were coughing on the streetcar in Min-
neapolis, Minnesota.
In Minocqua, Wisconsin, the girls kissed each other and
laughed,
The poison was working in Monroe, Illinois,
And in Stephanie, New Hampshire, burning fragments
were thrown up.

It was the day of the States, and from Topeka, Kansas,
To Lumberville, New York, trees were being struck
Down so they could put the platforms up. However I lay
struck
By sunlight on the beach at Waikiki, Hawaii . . .
Why can't Hawaii be one of the United States?
Nothing is being celebrated here; yet the beaches are
covered with sun . . .

Florida, Vermont, Alabama, Mississippi!
I guess that I will go back to the United States.
Dear friend, let's pack our bags and climb upon the
steamer!

36

Do not forget the birds you have bought in the jolly land
of France,
They are red white orange yellow green and pink and
they sing so sweetly,
They will make music to us upon the tedious ocean
voyage.

3

Tedious! How could I have said such a thing?
O sea, you are more beautiful than any state!
You are fuller and bluer and more perfect than the most
perfect action.
What is a perfect action?
In the streets of Kokomo a cheer goes up,
And the head of the lion is cursed by a thousand
vicissitudes.

Indiana! it is so beautiful to have tar in it!
How wonderful it is to be back on a trolley car, ding dong
ding!
I think I will wander into the barbershop and get my hair
cut!
Just hear the slice of the scissors, look at the comb!
Now to be once more out in the streets of Indiana
With my hair much shorter, with my neck smelling of
talcum powder!
O lucky streetcar wires to be able to look at me, and
through whom I can see the sun!

I did not know there was so much sun in North Dakota!
But the old man who is telling me about it nods his head
and says yes.

I believe him because my skin is peeling. Now I see
    people going to the voting booth.
The voting wagon is red and wooden, it stands on wheels
    where it is anchored to the curb.
I had no idea there were so many old men and old women
    in North Dakota,
But the old man who is explaining things to me says that
    each is above voting age.

4

I cannot remember what all I saw
In northern Florida, all the duck we shot.

You have asked me to recall Illinois,
But all I have is a handful of wrinkles.

Perhaps you would like me to speak of California,
But I hope not, for now I am very close to death.

The children all came down to see the whale in Arkansas,
I remember that its huge body lay attached to the side of
    the river.

5

O Mississippi joys!
I reckon I am about as big and dead as a whale!
I am slowly sinking down into the green ooze
Of the Everglades, that I feared so much when I was a
    child!

I have become about as flat as the dust on a baseball
diamond
And as empty and clear as the sky when it is just-blue
And you are three, and you stand on the rim of the zone
of one of the United States
And think about the forty-seven others; then in the
evening
Air you hear the sound of baseball players, and the splash
of canoes!
You yourself would like to play baseball and travel, but
you are too young;
However you look up into the clear flat blue of the
evening sky
And vow that you will one day be a traveler like myself,
And wander to all the ends of the earth until you are
completely exhausted,
And then return to Texas or Indiana, whatever state you
happen to be from.
And have your death celebrated by a lavish funeral
Conducted by starlight, with numerous boys and girls
reading my poems aloud!

6

O Charleston! why do you always put me in the mood for
kidding?
I am not dead yet, why do you make me say I am?
But I think I am growing older, my shoes are falling off,
I think it must be that my feet are getting thinner and
that I am ready to die.
Here comes my pony from Montana, he is a mere skull
and crossbones,

And here is the old man who told me about North Dakota,
    he is a little baby,
And here is Illinois, and here is Indiana, I guess they are
    my favorite states,
I guess I am dying now in Charleston, South Carolina.
O Charleston, why do you always do this . . . Gasp!
    Goodbye!

7

In Illinois the trees are growing up
Where he planted them; for he has died.
But I am the one who originally intended to read
You the fast movements. Now we will hear the *Branden-*
    burg
Concertos. Now we will go up in an
Airplane. Steady . . . The poet of America, Walt Whitman,
    is dead.
But many other poets have died that are reborn
In their works. He also shall be reborn,
Walt Whitman shall be reborn.

8

I did not understand what you meant by the Hudson
    Tunnel,
But now I understand, New Jersey, I like it fine,
I like the stifling black smoke and the jagged heave-ho of
    the trains,
I like the sunlight too at the end of the tunnel, like my
    rebirth in the poems of Kenneth Koch,

I like the way the rosy sunlight streams down upon the
    silver tracks,
I like the way the travelers awake from their dreams and
    step upon the hard paving stone of the station,
But I reckon what I should like best would be to see
    Indiana again,
Or Texas or Arkansas, or Alabama, the "Cotton State,"
Or Big Rose Pebble Island off the coast of Maine
Where I used to have so much fun during the summer,
    cooking and kidding and having myself a good time,
I like Pennsylvania too, we could have a lot of fun there,
You and I will go there when Kenneth is dead.

THE SCALES

Ann sat at the piano singing scales—
First the full-throated, evening-fated DO
(Self-consciousness to start at the right place
And get it low enough) and then the RE
With a slight rising, more secure by now
As to where in absolute sound that tone should fall;
Then, with dark half-disordered thoughts of self
Fighting from the the subconscious yet still willing
To be at last soothed by that music, MI;
Then with relief and a half smile breathed FA,
Then the demanding, round, full-throated SOL,
Which like the earlier note struck harmonies
In language not related to its place
In the parade of monosyllables,
Each with a tone; then, with eyes lighted, LA,
As if she had discovered something as
Delightful as the sound itself, yet more
Related to the world; then, scorning this,
A high, dry, light, and chiefly abstract TI
(Though thoughts were fighting here, despite the spelling,
And odors of hot smoke; but yet the struggle
Over the previous note made this one simpler
As a bright light distracts one from less light,
Or at least makes one capable of behaving,
Inspired, as if the lesser light weren't there,
One's eyes stung with the brightness of the other
And one's intention fortified by pain,
Defeat, and wish for purity; one has
The strength to go on there); at last a full,
Sweet-throated, evening-weighted, though much higher

Than that before it, more like afternoon
In just that moment when day turns to dark,
With pleasure at the ending, plus some strain
At feeling this impurity, oh full
Of all she had so far accomplished, DO.
Starting again, yet this time with the DO
With which she had concluded previously,
She sings it now, but weights it differently,
Which now is a beginning, not an end;
And, like the second step of the next flight
After the first, which leads one out of darkness,
Yet surely to a height one cannot go
Without divine assistance, she sings RE,
Which though it's higher than the last seems darker,
As if foreboding, still a lesser note;
Then, with more gaiety this time, a MI
That makes her think of roses, afternoons
When light is on the tea set, not so much
Conscious this time of an identity
As such, but an identity in things,
Or, rather, hovering round them—no, it's this:
This MI is a possible me sensed only in song,
Not hearty like the other with real doubt
Of earth and death; and now a lightsome FA,
Easy as feathers; then a trilling SOL
Which is to the last MI as is a detour
Which leads one to the sun; and then, as if
Song had no sound, one thrilling highest LA,
A whispered TI, and, coughing at the DO,
She clears her throat and starts this scale again,
Which she sings easily; a cool, clear TI
This time, and a high, lovely, round, full DO,
Like a small rose. Taking this rose again

She starts another scale with it; this time
A thrill is in her voice, for such beginning
Is dangerous, and she may never reach
The end of this third scale. Her confidence
In singing DO is balanced by a touch
Of gloom, or sign of strain, in the third RE,
And then a sense of real pain in the MI
(Self-consciousness, but now of a new kind—
As if she asked herself, "Can *I* do this?"),
Although it sings delightfully, then FA,
Attended by some tension toward its end
As if she felt she had to catch it up
And harden it, for fear that it would be
Too flabby-soft after what came before;
And then, with her whole spirit glowing, SOL,
Just right; and when, as on some garden steps
Whitewashed and lovely, one at last can see
The tulips washed above, blazing in red
And yellow, blue, and violet, and feels
Almost too weak to take those final steps
But yet is primed with energy by the beauty
That lies above, she mightily sang LA
(And here she gave up everything to God,
Or Fate, or chance, or Muses, or whatever,
And let her voice go, simply, if it would),
Then a delicious, light, high, spacious TI,
And, marvelous! one pure, celestial DO.
From this DO she descended: DO, TI, LA
(How strange it sounded, as if it were wrong!),
SOL, FA, MI, RE, DO!
Then down again from that relaxing DO
Quite in the middle: DO, TI, LA, SOL, FA
(Much easier, descending), MI, RE, DO;
Then taking up that DO again, still down,

And down again, DO, TI, LA, SOL, FA, MI,
RE, DO. And then, as if she wished to try
How deep her voice would go, she started DO,
TI, LA from there, but at the FA she choked,
Her face turned purple—something in her throat
Had split: she hemorrhaged; and, in three hours, died.

MA PROVENCE

En ma Provence le blé est toujours vert
Et les filles sont jolies
Elles ne meurent pas elles vous aiment à la folie—en ma
 Provence.

Bills break the breakfast teacups and the sun
Shines darkly over the bill-ware
She writes it out in enervating prose
"In my Provence, my rose."

COAST

Entwime this shower like a wave, cool elbows!
Amagansett syringe Calabria loop pajamas!
Total beloved flirt pool pajamas
Network sleep Anta photoplasm karmas.
Yes, I have Peruvian Tory plasmas!
Ope! evenings of arrogant dancing sleepies?
Cousin sylfur. Asleep? No.

How? Well, it's like this—
Pargis ulpy sleets at nine-pa
And show much to greep lah.
Toostoo? The gree da doomp cherry
It was three o'clock in the shah
But only nigh-den in the cours, ha?
On empulating. Shuzzup, he is dreenkp.
And,

Hoof morning dairy, alive, airy
Shahzump, has
"We cuzznt shay up too lade" cars
And fleas. Lem go kamma glurp. Ah,
Good morning! For nothing you expect
Shall interfere with this day's airy tines
To fork you music over heartfelt lines
If you can forget how tired we were last night.

Deceiving elf! Fazzum garra maggle twad. Enkh!
I should have known, cow mar a graceful beach stube,
    hats.
She lives here, appar, as in a throat
Buzz argam. Stop that, Tommy, I'm really awake!

Awake! awake! Azza magger gazump fazgul, eelmp
Oorp. Don't kid! I'm ready! See? Arzump.
And she appears
Attired in her beautiful white hair. *Dove e andata?*
Or, rather, *dove andiamo?* Rlzzzzzzzzzzzzzzzzzzz.

Chapter Forty. The Big Fish.
Then we went sailing, my taste duchess
End I, O frost unconscitude
Met, as agong puréed silver
Shazzle. Ooooohze, uhmp.
God dam somebody lib with.
Discovered silver.
Mahzgod limp.
Shoe.
Im-kazim.

Dear, wake up, we are—uh uh, no, ahzinnnnnnnng
Pajamas
Some panther azing Christ pajamas
Who to? not my sing? weeks, yes,
Entire frost go by
Before you'll wake up. . . . Himazzer beach
Izza grade painer—

O Puerto Com, goodbye!

SOME SOUTH AMERICAN POETS

JORGE GUINHIEME (1887–   )

BOILING WATER

The boiling water, Father, and princely teacher
Whose first reckoning with boiling water
The teeth of the far center will vindicate for seeds
Of us who have lost the first battle!
That boiling water is the dream
Of Jorge Guiells of the Civil Guard—
Every night he washes his passion in it,
Hoping that it will not rub off on the white ribs of Sevilla.
His mother watches him. With five ribs for screen
The dusty night darkens what he has willed.

CABANA AILANTHUS

At the Cabana Ailanthus when night breezes are stilled
One old commonwealth teacher remains fastened to his
    desk.
Through the night come the sounds of the frog
As if someone, or as if an entire people, had learned a
    Romance language.

OBSCURITY

When the dark night obscures of our tiny village the im-
    mense and topless steeple
Then we heard the bells ring out, for fear that some men
    might entrance not gain
To their preferred Eastern lights. But a fountain of anach-
    ronistic feathers
Darkens the blood of the priest gown before speechlessly
    he utter the ungracious words.

from THE STREETS OF BUENOS AIRES
ROSEWAY

O unfeigned laughter of a fine young girl—
Or even of one not so fine—
Young girl, that is the essential thing,
And laugh unfeigned—
But how can you not be fine beneath your roses?

CABANA DE TURISTAS, CALLE DE SUENOS (DREAMS)

Here, where there are tourists
Gathered, let us carry
From one of them to another
The money from their country
That they may see
We do not wish it for ourselves
But only that they may share with one another
What they have.

PLEASURE STREET

When all are sleeping
The staccato of those not sleeping
Is a mysterious graph on which
The mathematics teacher studies nightly
To find the stars.

CALLE ROSA

Roseway, oh lovely girl,
Your face is like a tulip.
I have tulip * too, my lovely girl,
And happily will mingle them with yours.

---

* "Tulip" is in English in the original.—*Trans.*

50

from STREETS
More open to the light
Than many little streets
This one on which I met you
Carrying a basket of light
To the sea, is my preferred one of
All the little by-ways of the city.

Luis de Calliens (1918–   )

CANCION DE NOCHE
A catacomb of feathers
Boiling. A frame.
The steep frame of ducks' loves roiling
Together the fantastic pathways.

Now a drumstick of night,
Two Indians on a highway—
One stricter than a feather,
The other, clasped by might.

TO A DREAM
Chuckle out, great planned song
Of the ages!
Laugh ages henceforth to be so free!
We are the ones who knew you in
Your star-spangled babyhood—
We are the perusers of your eternal rose!

THE MORGAN LIBRARY
I, Luis de Calliens, Spanish teacher
And South American poet, as I am known,
See now in Nueva York this Morgan Library
Spattered by the mutual funds of her bloody night.
The rich in Nuena de Cangias do not build libraries
And the poor carry a network of berries into the future's
    light.

LUIS CARIGES (1922–   )

PERIPHER-ARGENTINE
How many stories, bought from love and rain,
This testimony winks to see. Above
These Herculean heights,
Peripher-Argentine,
And far above the desecrated woodlands
And the hopeless farmlands
And the testimonials of bright Western night
A human voice begins a styptic melody
Corroded by your blossoms
Indifferent to the month
And year of every star—
O Argentine!

BESOS
My mouth, a cascade of kisses!
And, purely below me, your mouth too,
An equal cascade of remembrance, farms of bliss,
Evidence, preoccupation, evening stars,
Truly, reversing our tables,
When, at dusk, we reform
Trees to their original grandeur,
As nude as each other's stars.

MUSIC
A song creates its own music.

Juan Garcia (1940–   )

O rolling mountains of my native fascist unconscious
    mother!
O divine transcendence of some future impassioned
    stream!
When the souls of the billionaires shall lie streaming in
    the bloodied
Banknotes of a whorish fantasma, whose plucked grace
    notes the hideous transactor no longer
Imbues with the maleficent horror of death's magnificent
    scream!

What, O rolling native mountains whose fascist resistances
Strike against the mutinied hearts of mothers, of orphans,
    of knees
Of silence, what are your invocations, to me, and to my
    mother poets,
What emblems do you carry for us? when shall we strike
    the DOLLARO from the hideous mustang of our
    homes?

ODE TO GUINHIEME

When shall we strike the dollaro, magnificent poet, be-
    trayer of your class?
When shall we tear the mould-headed thread-ribbed
    dollaro to pieces?
Speak, Guinhieme, if you know . . . but you do not know,
    and you will not speak. You spew wildly into your
    lunch!

VACTHA (193?–)

CAMPANHO
Roll, little garden fields, away!
No longer the garden, they insist
As proper for a muse. This time, however, once peruse
The mist and that fair fountain
Which is reflected there
As in the early starlight
Over Buenos Aires
It begins to rain.
First drops!

TORCITO
Brilliant little baby, walk
Across the portico. There, a smiling mama
Will take you in her arms. You will smile.
And I too shall smile. And in this poem I shall enshrine
    you forever!

The essence of Argentinian poetry is the *hasos,* or fallen limb. I do not know if my English readers will get a clear idea of this structural element of poetry without some further words of explanation. *Hasosismo,* or the "art of the fallen limb," a technique which was buried deep in the history and classicism of the poetry of our Argentine, is recently brought into the foreground by works of masters who have seen what long was hidden, that to be authentically new the poet is obliged to find poetic elements which are authentically old—that is, authentically *his own.* For we do not exist in the new, but in the permanent—where all is both old and new—and it is the poet's task precisely to remind us of this condition. The "art of the fallen limb," insofar as it can be separated from the Argentinisms of prosodic and syllabic ramifications, may be, I suppose, briefly said to be *the art of concealing in one line what has been revealed in the previous line.* Younger practitioners and, above all, explicators of the *hasosismo* have made often the error of seeing this function as the reverse of what it actually is: the revelation in one line of what was concealed in the preceding—or, the concealing in one line of what is to be revealed in the next. This is not hasosismo: this is fancy and the commonest and most ordinary of poetic and all narrative processuses. HASOSISMO IS THE MYSTERY OF NIGHT COVERED BY THE DAY; IT IS NOT THE DAY, WHICH IS REVEALED AFTER BEING HIDDEN IN THE NIGHT. The difference here is one of heights to plains. San Baz has *hasosismo;* Cediz does not. Juanero is a million miles from having it. In Batorje it is supreme.

GUINHIEME[*]

* *Hasosismo* is difficult to illustrate, since by its very nature it tends to cover its own tracks. Furthermore, in translation much is necessarily to be lost, but the attempt is worth making, since this heartstone of poetry deserves to be known beyond our language. Here are some examples from the middle work of Batorje:

> The streets of the city are shining, wet with light
> In the dark and dry forgetfulness of rivers . . .
>> *Motion of Trees* (1932)

> You give me your hand; it is white with pointed
> Forests accepting the horizon . . .
>> *Moon Breed* (1936)

> We stand in clouds. The highest tree, far beneath us
> Our underwater stamina muddies toward her true
>> contempt.
> Indians once walked along this grit with plastic bells
> Whose trees only her final simplicity can chide . . .
>> *Modern* (1943)

In San Baz can be found experiments in using the *hasos* within the line, rather than in succeeding lines. The inspiration from Batorje seems self-evident:

> Sweet dreams! dry daylight sounds without feeling or
>> image—
>> SAN BAZ, *October on the Railroad* (1960)

> I look at you. Oceans of beer gush from the left side
> of my collar bone.
>> SAN BAZ, *Madam* (1964)

Garcia, in attempting to use the *hasos* politically, has, I think, essentially weakened its poetic function, but some of his examples have a notable strength:

The Fascists have tied up their mistresses:
One set of brawny men kicking another in the teeth!

> JUAN GARCIA, *The Mistresses of Garcia* (1962)

They have befouled us
With the perfumes of exultation.

> JUAN GARCIA, *Homage* (1964)

Calliens, in perhaps too academic a way, has praised the *hasos* in verses using it themselves. Of the long (200 lines) poem, these verses are characteristic:

A small brain, you are a wide heart;
A great inspirer, you seek only liquids;
Sainthood, O Hasos, the bed-land of America!
A street without silence, you are the steel one;
My heart without drama, you pet the mammal dog;
O Hasos, my clear observation!

> CALLIENS, *In Praise of Hasos* (1961)

An example of what *hasos* is NOT, though it has sometimes been thought to be:

A dark congregation of valleys
Suddenly brings us the sea.

> LUIS CEDIZ, *Atalanta* (1943)

From my own work, in conclusion, two examples, one of which I believe to have the *hasos,* the other not:

The dark pagan of the sea
Rolls endlessly into our childhood . . .

> *Flavinia* (1936)

Mountains reverberate; seas roar
For the Christhood in which they believe.

> *Otros Cristos* (1957)

J.G.

Hasosismo in a pure state mocks the punditism of the masters. Guinhieme's "hasosismo" is no more the pure form that appeared in Lope than is Guilha's "structured license." Neither modern writer has bothered to do his scholarship well. Both have confused a linguistic particularity with a technic structure of design.

Hasosismo, as we encounter it in Lope and in certain of his contemporaries, is no more than a fixed, and academically fixed and predetermined way of avoiding the vulgar and over-explicit in every instance. One characteristic function of this kind of esthetico-literary lèse-majesté is the avoiding of revealed nakedness, a gently clothing over of all that is too barely and openly flung before the reader's eyes.

In Gomero and Pepite this one aspect of true *hasosismo,* which to Guinhieme is *hasosismo* itself and entire, was stressed at the expense of the whole and true concept, which no longer seemed to fit an age of vulgarity and expansion. Gomero's "hasosismo" was the artist's replique to a time which he found too vulgar to share his concerns and certainly his visions. The thing stated was immediately hidden: it is an art of the standstill. We feel the anguish of his time in this technique.

This is not all of *hasosismo.* To Guinhieme and to others of a modern time, a time which feels itself more anguished perhaps than that of a Gomero or a Pepite, this one use of *hasosismo* necessarily appeals. The mistake is forgiven as soon as it is understood. But the term is vulgarized in the process. Of all the foci of Argentine esthetics it is this one (*hasosismo*) which it most imports, perhaps, to retain in purity. For true *hasosismo* has reference to both diction and structure. Without this knowledge the student of Lope is fatally handicapped before he has begun.

OMERO PECAD, *Studies for a Leftist University*,
Buenos Aires, 1963.

HOMAGE

A long line of lyricists
Starting with Lope
Move toward the station —
Listen to them shouting!
Look at their breeziness!
They have befouled us
With the perfumes of exultation!

Listen to them praising!
Whom do they praise now?
Francisco Franco!
Demagogues and Popes!
Look at them grazing!
What do they feed on now?
Aspirations, hopes!

Ah let us destroy them
Immediately!
Cut up their breeches!
Turn them into baloney!
Feed them to the pigs, when
Darkness is approaching!
Lyricist! Hash! Over here!

JUAN GARCIA

OCTOBER ON THE RAILROAD

A pure blue sun in the sky! the red leaves fall.
Some of the yellow ones are still holding on to their
    branches.

And in the distance I hear the engine roar.
October on the railroad! Sometimes, like a rhinoceros,
Fierce and angry, the gray locomotive will come
Tearing the leaf-beds to pieces, and at other times
The engine is gentle, a lakeside hotel
Perhaps, where one's mistress is staying.
One longs to see her—is it a dream?
Sweet dreams! dry daylight sounds without feeling or
    image
Consult the atlas of a goodbye! And now the train!
Will it take me to Switzerland, do you think? Bavaria?
That depends, O stems, upon your road . . .

GARCIA SAN BAZ

MADAM

I look at you. Oceans of beer gush from the left side of
    my collar bone
And down my sides, until they form a crystal pool at my
    feet
In which children are swimming. I push them back and to
    one side.
Perhaps to love you only it has been given
To me, lady beyond many sorrows. Perhaps you are not of
    the Mistresses of Garcia
Or of Streets Which Are Waving Goodbye. But I love you.
    Straw sailors
Come out of my brow. They coast in that fresh sea sky.

GARCIA SAN BAZ

MEADOWS

Prairies outside dormant cities, America of dreams!
There is no reason for you to be without collarbone.
Without dentistry, yes, they have killed him many times,
But not the definitive movies which showed him rolling
In a pirate flag uphill. No, I am not explaining
Too much. I think you walk quietly to me.
Do you remember what our feeling was
Before we took positions up? Then, quietly walking over
Was all we asked of life. Perhaps the days
Were shorter then, though they are not long now.
Perhaps the only thing we said was Yes
To a dreamy tyrant who has enslaved us now
In the boughs of a tree. The pig raved and slept.
In trains we have been shorter than our pampas.

GARCIA SAN BAZ

SEINE

Hounded by Central Islip till the end
Of pyrethmetic days, and onward wishing
Oh that he like me and she like me too,
And the green arboretum bush waving
And the elephant in his noose waving
And the deaths saying goodbye—
Hello to the Death Family!
Here is mother, father, and here is Nell:
She is looking very bright and pretty in her nasturtiums
And the sea wall caves down—
Exit Roland with Angelica *in braccia: Come?*
Says Orlando, you expect to find a bathroom
In these mountains? Come on, now, father, now.
And the Greece temperature change index that day
Floogled all the way bottom to a chortled bottom,
I began to rain confidence on the eastern shore
When the Egyptian confidence room opened, she looked
     pretty
She had him eating nasturtiums out of a symbolic tube
Of yesterday's restored brush-stroke emblems, whose
Pie only God could call a "more than gift."
There were selected ways and "island gift"
And "party pris" and all other conduct emblems
Toward a future and then toward a future
And then her neck toward a future—if you call "the
     limited way."
And maybe after all that is right. Maybe the alert dock
     hound
Scimitar evening is "frigolescent"—I think you look pretty
With me; she had him call in hallways
With busted floors, and when he gave the album

Of wasted flowers to her mother, she
Began to dance, as if Okie's Delicatessen were shifted
    Paris.
But cannot come easily to the true meaning,
Which is "he topped her puberty"? No,
Another bale to want about Ann Jeffries.
Then she began to slip up, down the beaches
Where cookies had been laid. To her the colonel
Was just a human mattress, but the sea
Was dialectic brilliance. They all lived family
Style in a huge straw hut in the Barbados
Where Dad worked out fifteen hours a day as a steward
In a psychiatric shipping firm
Down St. Louis Avenue. Melanie took up the fluffy powder
And smashed it into the clothesline towel. Damn Bernie,
She said. And the ocean keeps flashing
Signs of hope, or "perfection is a bottle of iced tea"
As the lost ranger said, when Uncle Ernie
Was smashed to doom beside the oceanic cave
And Martha came back to her babies above land, with
    this sad news.
Come on, Ariel, I'm tired of dippy
Parties and your slow-down repartee.
There is only one great comic born every five million
    "antons," said Uncle Ernie,
But Pam said, "You're the ivory lord, of me."
And the balls were hit out into the infield
And the outfield, and Bernie kept looking for the
Ball which Bettie had hit which had a white necktie
    painted on it
And he said There is only one great comic born every five
Million "epons," it was impossible to see the Mediter-
    ranean
In her waving bush, since Fred had deleted the ikons

From the coffee machine. I began to catch on at last, and
    opened,
Myself, a King Kong Fruit Store. We have
A great comic among us, Beirut Radio said—
You who are truly my friend would never welcome
A personal appearance that betrayed me like this one
For no sooner had the beautiful wolfhound princess en-
    tered the Microbe Hotel
But that Dr. Factory began to strut and scratch. He said,
    Welcome
To fruit-bar, but Edna was so cold
From being in the bottle plant, and the Ant Riviera was
    closed
For feeding period, so there was nothing
To do but come out clothed as ducks,
Which is what we did, and which caused the trouble
You are hearing about now in the radio report
From Radio Free Biarritz which I have on my cufflinks
As a kind of "Sunday emblem," which you are,
In fact, committed to no more than lightning,
But lightning which populates the future
Still can leave a frigid old cow in Banff
And so I say Let all the images stored up by the flashing
    towels
Be a passionate party to that ship's constant loneliness
As it triples its fuels by emptying one pale guitar—
Unless you are synthetic and can drop silver from gold.
The Medicine Man told me. As a cow drops into the
    future
From the past. He smiles. The bettered ivory on the keys
Begins to braise her eyes with some Smetana,
And she turns toward the grizzled orphan with a cuss-
    word

Standing on the lips of the cornflakes which she has
    brought you from the mountains
Where the answer was found, by one old goat, in her
    lipstick.
Smear, smear, said the old Bavarian gush-hound;
And let us too smear the ways
Of this dachshund hemorrhage Rapunzel ivory princess
Who promises everything and does everything for the
    profit
Of two long ivory staves, which she finds in the mountains
So that when after the sun has set the ship is still there
And all preparations are being made for the werewolf to
    collapse in a movie,
Still there is the dead stock-still response of the whispering
Of the sea, and the flat land past desire. America
Remembers it, an orange, pubescent with desire. The old
Doctor disremembers it, and pulses with a swallow-tail
    recuperation. "Day is yet nigh!"
"The night is yet harmless!" "Nameless, oh you, all-
    absorbent!"

The spoons, though puzzled, in surprise mentioned the
    baccalaureate
To the weak Mexican town, who, immediately nestling
With a coccyx-less elephant, defied them to repeat it
    on the
Horse, which they did next day, unrelenting,
Until Venice had to be thoroughly searched for a powder
    to dry
When their noggins began to wink, stirred by the future
    excellence
Of tiled oil-catchers, which, when they were ferreting
The priests kept dumping into their unused viola da
    gambas

Notched for excellence, and purple violins when they
    went prinking
About the outskirts for these reeds pure notices of choice
To the intelligences of the Rapunzels of another era;
My own selection from the feed of heaven is climate,
Choice, and the feed of these heavenly bars
Which the oysters strafed all night above the climate
Which was making these bars drive crazy, and apes and
    chimpanzees
Also into the reputed gulf which—here he was inter-
    rupted
By a change of powder. Nutmeg Carson has gotten in the
    game!
These jewels which the boat slips through the water
And which are reputed "nephew" "palfrey" and "hem"
Still could have been manufactured by a greater
Emblem than your poor dope of a cloud.
If these passionate sleeves fondled colors in choices
Until the civics absolutely went another way
Then there are ices and sleeps and aloes—
The dwarf is a greater man; but the heap is a greater.

Now one old general comes here to say
His prayers above the city. Someone is dropped into a
    crater
And here someone Egyptian goes to sleep. An idiot is born
    in Parigi,
And an ivory stove is wheezed about in Paris. A man
    begins to cry
At the thought of the baby, and a woman begins to grieve
At the formation of an intelligence without a nerve.
Closer together, the humorless blossoms can signify
Only the return peanut of a mateless tennis match—
How curious to be dead beneath a sky

68

In which everything remarkable is hidden—except for
the flocks
Of the birds, and an occasional Numa
(Someone's name), blue jewels, and the raucousness of
grasshoppers
Closing the jalousies into Olga Park
Where the bunnies lie about like extreme craters
Strewn by the cashiered parallax of jolting
When there were no more tears in the canal.
And now a baby brings an apple. The rabbi sleeps.
The hirsute rainbucket of phosphorescence is decapitated
By the coolness of a sigh—or by the cruelty of a lamb.
It is right, but the secret was before
On the left, and before the end of last month
She played with a jewel. Now, in the winter, it is removed
from her mouth
Where an ice hockey game dropped the calves of the
girls' legs
So far below freezing the defilade deprived me of the
right to wish that it was not my chopper
But the sea that was going down.

Maybe it is a land of oblongs
For which you have been pining all your days
Next to the stove museum where Ann brought Henry
And said Look at the clouds, Henry; see how the sky plays
Tricks with the ordinary person's vision; and Henry's
okeys
Surprised the madam because they were so sheer,
So useless, finally, for understanding
If he liked the glass dales or not, because he had been
tempted
Previously to renounce the bluish black top hat which
she had

Purchased for him Saturday midnight the Giudecca
He said I needn't look so good in that
As you suppose, or as chiffon supposes. The sea
Was turgid with fuming tumescence; it was squealing
Like an itemized tribune of flatulent glass dolls and kisses
Through a chimney, in the skyway, or lip outline mark
Where the dollar bills first established their mastery
Always coming down on the fir tree seeking white bread
Which the farmer had promised them in some distant
    time
Before the pure colonnades existed, at the left was the
    laundry
And on the right was the sty—there was a continual *va
et vient*
Between the two columns of porphyry,
A nicety for when the purple-coated monster apples did
    come
Bearing a pension for the silence, which she hated.

It is moonlight now
Over the bears.
Father Bear is tired, and he says to Mother Bear,
"The island is becoming too small for our twelve little
    fishing boats;
I would like to establish a concession on the mainland,
    which would like
To concede me oblongs." Mother Bear hopped about in
    the silence
Of the fresh blue air, and she glanced at Father
Over her shoulder. He looks like a Catholic priest, she
    imagined,
Or, as when I first saw him dancing in Yugoslavia,
He looks like Judas Priest. And Mamma Bear said, "Wor-
    thington,

Worthington, you have been on the island too long;
It is time for us to think about the little ones,
The everpresent and omnivorous baby bears,
Who are coming up every year as a result of our screwing,
Of them we must think and of bear job opportunities
Which I agree would be greater on the mainland."

I grow tired of this absurd simplicity as quickly as you do,
But it represents the truth. If bears' concerns
Are not exactly identical with human ones,
Yet it's only by human analogies that we can understand
    them.
She placed a red hot moccasin on the table and was gone.

A difference between me and you—
You are abjectly hopeful in a steamy kind of way,
Whereas I am pure flawed crystal, able to share my light
With a universe which is pure flawed eyeball. I wonder at
The exaggerations to which occasions force
You; and I marvel
At the bracelet which you bring
Into the charmed circle of the bullfight when you say:
"The test of prudence is a life of need
To spend outside the Bauhaus. It is kind,
But not imprudent, to attack with a certain variety of
    orange rind
The devastate vicinity canals—I've got that wrong—
The deadly fascination of canals—no, that's wrong
    either—
Devastating vicinity of canals
Is what I meant, but that is not right anyway
Since 'what I mean' is never what I meant
Except in some inferior phosphorous sense

Which includes the twelve meanings of the verb 'to be.'
    Are you still listening—?"
And you go on and on and on
And I am still listening because I marvel at what you say,
They are my own thoughts exactly, I have been dead for
    six years
And you have been bearing high the red torch of tra-
    dition,
You alone are doing it, there is no one else—
Well, put it down, I am coming back to life,
I am tired of living in the earth and dishes
A little blue rabbit has been doing the dishes
And I am longing for the turtles,
The turtles of fascination which I once saw on the plates,
And the rabbit hearts that vanished from the piers.

Perhaps it is the wrong word, kindness,
For the revolting way we treat each other
On Fridays and Sundays, though on Saturday night
All seems to be going well, the doorbell the incinerator
The childish rat; and you lean over a parking bench to
    say,
It is well, that the clouds smeared with ugliest cinnamon
    mirror
An "exuberant" sky, then said that was the wrong word,
Shyness, for the way we act about the dwarf
In the white suit, who is always going into the coast
Food station as if it were a mixture
Of paradise and the seven brassieres' hell. A mystery to
    awaken
Some morning would be this fluting, which is constantly
    imperceptible
Although the roofs do their insane best not to resist it,
And you at last are well away on the trail

Which you love. Even the little pears could not prevent it
Nor the giant apples lying across the trail. They said, You
    need a building,
A large one, a canoe hut diverged with apple blossoms;
We smiled at the old wet men and went our way
Toward the wet women; each had been alive at least
    thirty years;
The parking beach was deserted; a kind of crisscross
Of flags and passageways could doubt the trees' maturity;
A single person could never become transparent on that
    beach;
The days shove under; a millionaire leaves his legs
For the benefit of science; the car fashion institute is
    roped in
By delicate oblongs. Some slow marble clickings drift
    unconsciously toward the sea
Of idiotic markings, made by a change
In the weather, from red to chlorine swill. My aunt,
The Countess of Freitagen, always used to call it
"The cruelest animal," because of the way it behaved
In a stiff collar, although the dirtiest water
Could never find it to put its foot in it in the silly
Repeating islands. There at least we had a chance to gasp
And sunbathe for fifteen seconds, just then the monsoon
Began to collect its annual tariff of ptomaine animals and
    teacups
Which the frizzled breeze was flinging into the channels
Of a poodle's heart, whose master was a mistress
Of fortunate clouds—that day, lay pink and white and
    chuckled
Out, the sweet men of the sea. To harm this legion
Jessica accounted a heinous crime, but Beo-grime was
    redundant

With ectoplasmic gripes. Look, he said, this whole silence
    of the tundra
As measured with a fish's thigh, sheer global
Different acrimony—how high can you go in a canoe?
    And Julian said,
That would depend on your astronomy. Both brothers
    leaped into the *Please Me*
And rose high over the lumps of dough which Fish-Bath
    had left spread about the co-stars
Whose names Tim took rapidly writing down—Amos,
    Ben, and Sandy, which one is the girl?
Tim kept pondering the question all day long;
Then, that night, the hugest egg was laid
That ever Parma's vegetables had witnessed.
My cheese came down from the fuel-indoctrinating moun-
    tains to witness
For itself the enticing event of pure white docks above the
    habitable
Tennis shoes, ever tired of renouncing.
Then, suddenly, the sea began to play for assembly
And even the dunce was astonished. Long previously, the
    white fantastic ballroom
Had been imperceptibly vanishing from the cookies'
    carnival
Of dishwatered kisses, and then she replied The canal.
It was cook's water and old light feeding the empire
Once again, beside the faded bricks. She took a peacock's
    tail and set sail
Up to the dormitory window, where Peter
Had left the emulsion to savagely rest. Juliet, who had
    been wintering by the phosphate,
Then crushed Olson with a dream. Her purse opens.
In it we see sea monsters of every variety
And this includes the fabulously terrifying sea apples

Which the district attorney of cloud beds was so studi-
ously refurbishing
Above the lacy dormer windows when I cried in bed
About the horror of the flowers and the flies. Jules said:
The infection
Will not last past morning; the defeated island
Now brings its crazy promise to the head-rows of the sea.
A boat slapped
Against the knee-farmer's tail. It was summer. The glass
cloudburst
Had finished by breaking the records of the first clouds—
Of which these islands proudly led the way into the tea
shop.

Inside every animal is a beleaguered Shanghai man,
Said Frederick the First of Prussia. We in our modern day
Are fond of the brushwork quotation. We think that pro-
tects us from the apples.
It was Gabriel d'Annunzio, was it not,
At the time of his tragic love affair with Sarah Bernhardt—
Unless it was with some other great star that he had this
affair, Duse?
It was d'Annunzio who said—I have forgot
Whate'er d'Annunzio said. The night is hot.
Come, let's go out into its feverish breeze.
We wandered into a hay station and bar. You had a gin
and orange.
I looked at the stable part of the atmosphere discon-
solately.
This ambience, I said, 's no *ambiance*—aye, there's a
difference, let me tell it to you,
Aye, there's a difference to the heart again.
The summer foamed with released past time memories
and golden heart-attack fundromes

Where the egregious eagles could play at shibboleth and
    night's pastime violin.
The crushing night was sounding
As if the sea were full of air,
And as if some boat came pounding
Along the entire coast looking for a single hair.
A wiry one, I'll warrant; better clues
They make, those wiry ones. He put his shoes
Into the dashboard refrigerator and cleft Yugoslavia
Into the shape of a sloe-eyed button. You must not go
    there, she said
With a college horse; take along a necktie for his button.
In the winter the clouds gave the heart attack a purse
Of wishes—one of the wisest of these was to play the
    guitar
With an ikon's shrieking delight. But summer, spring, and
    fall met at once, with great plans for rebellion.
"Oblongs will never be our treat tonight,"
Villa said; but Harry saith,
"Oblongs are going to be our treat tonight."

THE INTERPRETATION OF DREAMS

1

You are my Sweetheart
Sang the tin can
I was sitting on a truck
As it rolled along
You are my Truck
Sang my Sweetheart
Somehow it was menacing
An ominous song
I hardly knew what to say I went into the truck
It was amazing
That autumn afternoon, when every affection came un-
      sought
As from an unstoppered lute and a glass of campari
Was downed from a shimmering glass and quickly as if
      nothing
Could harm the eternal beaver any more. But a policeman
      of high reflection
Suddenly stood up for the traffic crossings' protection
And were we sad, lost in thought at our newfound abor-
      tionlessness
In stages, because of a green kerchief stuck in your
      pocket
As one asks What's the difference between that and a
      handkerchief? and
Between each stop and its parenthesis? Let's assume we
      have too much
And pound on the marble table top. It has always gone
      best that way

Yet you're thinking (I think) "Yet the hand falls off
And the streets of Paris will continue to go every which
    way.
No, in spite of your palaver
And a summertime gift for describing the rose
You will have to take me into another valley
Where reality is not affliction." Or if you did not think
    that all at once
Toward that our thoughts have been gathering. Whose
    omnibus is that parked outside the S. S. Rose
With a Himalayan flagboy in the window of the car
Scratching his initials A.H., A.H., as the winter evening
    dies
And turns into a springtime fogbound morning? I was
  sleeping in the hay
When we awoke. One could just barely make out the sky.
    A truck raced past.
Then I realized where we were. It was potato season.
    And, Spiff! this season was to be our last
Before we dangled before tomatoes, hard red ones and
    yellow yummy
Tomatoes and huge hard pink ones which were brighter
    than the nose
Of Snow White in Walt Disney's fiction. I am going into
    slaveland
To help these tomatoes get free, but they come thumping
After. "Wait for us! Wait! You will see! It is impossible to
    serve us unless we are there!"
And the tomatoes turned into apples. I was wide awake.
    The cook said, "You are my Sweetheart."
And a band played "The Abortion of the Sleeper may be
    the Swan Song of the Sheep-Man's Heart."

2

Into this valley my sweetheart came
The tomatoes were hard as her nose
She was available exactly
Five minutes every afternoon
Then she took Snow White
Into the kidney parlor
She said "Snow White, be an actress!"
And Snow White implored the yellow movies
To be more reasonable about Al Capp
"He's a swell guy"
We know we know
But he's not purple anymore
A large picture flew through the sky
My Sweetheart put on it
"I am the Capistrani of the Rose"
And William Butler Yeats died
When Auden wrote the poem
About the deftness of the steamship
Plying through the harbor
Is my Sweetheart's nose.

3

Meanwhile Snow White and her boyfriend
Have gone up into the mountains.
It is amazing what they will do for a game of bingo!
No! That is not what they are doing. Look!
They are making love! I didn't know that was allowed in
    the movies
In this country! But that must be what they are doing!

She is lying beneath him and every time his body rose
I saw her fingerprints gripping the dust like the U.S.S.
    Idaho
In an old story. Do you know the one of the Frightening
    Fidget?
Well, in this one old Doctor Barnose
Is riding along through Italy on a great white highway
Made of marshmallows, when some greensuited police-
    men come out
And make him stop to show his passport, which he had
    had made out of clothes
As a modern novelty, but they threw him in the purple
    prison,
Where like an Italianate tirade of grapejuice something
    exists to this day
Numbered among the aquanauts who saved this country
From being bombed by the submarines which I pur-
    chased you for my birthday
In one of my most powerful moods, on the Pomeranian
    coast.

4

The gasoline must come to a halt, as the great apple ship-
    ments have done.

The true Advisor to the lesser party will not permit the
    Eczema to come
Into the park of Dutiful Silence. This is an Order imposed
    by Law.

The Marlene Dietrich suitcases are not to be opened

Except by the pink hands of the Prelate in charge of the
bombing.
(Cardinal Spellman, I am dreaming of you! I am seeing
your plumpness insulted by bombs!
And then I am seeing the grass-green acne of the trends.)

In charge of fishes Israel is put; in charge of Packaging,
Summer.
(I am sorry, Winslow Homer, that you did not get this job,
And you, yearning seminarians of our Hungarian Pall
Mall,
But it is a direct icing I get, and not a "forwarded," from
the Divine.)

And now I think it is time to cut out Music.

5

The musicians are viciously bald. They will not listen to
the music
Whether it is good or bad. They say, "Oklahoma has taken
the best music. And then Snow White. We have noth-
ing left."
They laugh, the musicians, at their own sorrow.
But at least the music has stopped.
I hated the music, it was always resounding in the ears
Like a broken fiddle. I am glad you have imposed on them
to stop.
It was of their own free will, like the other decisions
They have made, like which fish to have on Wednesday
And how to catch mackerel without a rod. I am tired now
of "not hearing" the music
In such a lively way. Can we go down to the harbor?

In the harbor everything was a bad job.
The courts were out of work and the community centers
      were filled with people
Eating pastry-cakes shaped like sheets of music. "All those
      good pies," I said,
"Being wasted like a nuthouse." And I run rampant.
I rock around smashing everything I could find.
They had destroyed my darling and I was going to ruin
      them as well.
Then struck the clock. It was the time of the oyster and
      the octopus.
I walked out of the fishstore with a prayer.
The universe was ringing with a song.

6

Snow White had brought the music back.

7

The yo-yo capitalists are filled
By the pastry which tyrants heat
On Mediterranean ovens.
You now feel that you will never understand;
But it is about to open, becoming easy
As one may say "Ah!" at the sight of a pink island
Or a tremendous pink apple which is of a different kind
From every other apple one has ever tasted
And as Snow White
Who had an island pedigree in black and white
Came ravished when in colors.

A new hydrofoil has started
To invent the sea. And when the sea comes in
The birthday poem is finished and a nude start begins
On some fantastic island—"Fantastic island?" I'll never
    question you any more.
But sexuality is not all, even though it is beautiful
As Moravian gusts. One also needs a spellbinding heart
And a lethal spelling book, which gives the Seminole
    report.

"I'm in love with apples,"
The old seminarian says.
But the young Arethusa knows better:
"Alpheus is in love with me."

8

Oh American homerun hitter! your balls! your balls!
They are sailing over our trees
And when they land
We feel we pick up a killer
Oh American homerun hitter
Dressed in white tie and tails!

And you smote your guitar
Good cousin Jute with a loud report.
"This is America! This is the Capitalist country
Where witnesses write on the trees
And black meets white
In a catapult, blast, and explosion. It is not Nude Island."

"So what?" said the caterpillar, and

"So what?" whispered the trees. From every direction the
	"so-whatters" came running
To compel him to retain his distance.
The porkchop and the shark said
"If you come too close to us, we die.
Remember the speech of the living.
And welcome back to Thorax Island."

Then a picture of Snow White completely blocked out
	the sky.

9

And I was with you again
But we were going in different directions.
We met and started to go in the same direction.
Then once more our paths crossed and we met again
Under the believable blue of a traffic light where we had
	first met
The village coconut who had forbidden our meetings
But now we meet all the time.
"You go this way and I'll go that,
And when we head back we will meet
And declare our love."

This is the foundation of the emotions.
The sky is our parade ground and our glove.
The fish in the bay are the slaves of their time and not
	of art
But somehow our emotions can become their emotions.
This is the beginning of Realism. This is the end of the
	ideal.
This is the degree of front and back.

EQUAL TO YOU

Can you imagine the body being
The really body the being the reality
Body being the body if reality
Is what it is it is, not that reality
Doesn't infer the body, still
The body being the bearer of reality
And the barer of the body
The body being reality
That is reality's reality
Hardly on earth ever seen
But from it we have the word *connubial*
Which means
The body bearing the body in reality
And reality being the body
And body-reality being borne.
I am bearing a burden
Which reminded me of you
Bearing away the swell
Of the sea
But can you imagine the body bearing reality
And being reality
That's where we get the
Word *connubial* which is a word for the body's being
Being in reality and being a body
In reality and bearing the burden
Of the body in reality, by being real
And by being the body of the real.

FACES

The face of the gypsy watching the bird gun firing into
   the colony of seals; but it was filled with blanks;
The face of the old knoll watching his hills grow up before him;
The face of the New England fruit juice proprietor watching his whole supplies being overturned by a herd of
   wild bulls;
The face of a lemur watching the other primates become
   more developed;
The face of gold, as the entire world goes on the silver
   standard, but gold remains extremely valuable and
   is the basis for international exchange;
The face of the sky, as the air becomes increasingly filled
   with smoke and planes;
The face of the young girl painted as Saint Urbana by
   Perugino, whose large silver eyes are focused on the
   green pomegranate held by a baby (it is Jesus) in
   the same painting;
The face of the sea after there has been a storm, and the
   face of the valley
When the clouds have blown away and it is going to be
   a pleasant day and the pencils come out for their
   picnic;
The face of the clouds;
The faces of the targets when all the arrows are sticking
   out of them, like tongues;
The face of insects; the tiny black moustachioed inepti-
   tude of a fly;
The face of the splinters on the orange crate;
The face of the Depression, which shook up America's
   faith in her economy so badly;

86

The face of President Hoover during this event;

The face of Popeye; the face of Agamemnon; the face of
    Ruth in the Bible; the face of Georges Simenon;

The face of the hornet; the face of the carnation; of the
    orchid; the face of the roots of the elm tree;

The face of the fruit juice stand proprietor in Hawaii—it
    is black and lined

With the years and the climate; the face of God in Pintu-
    ricchio; the 1920's face of Gala Eluard;

And the face of Paul Eluard; the face of the birthday
    party as envisioned by Pablo Picasso; the map of
    Ireland

In Barbara's face; the map of Egypt on the wall

Of the Alexander-of-Macedon-looking hotel proprietor's
    face; the eye's face; the face of the ear; faces of all
    the noses;

The face of the snowman; the face of Rome

In being Mistress of Europe (if she was) in the fifteenth
    century;

The nude in her environment with sketched-in face

Or suggested face; the magic face of the chestnut tree

Blowing in the wind and scattering its teeth; the face of
    the bachelor's button; the face of the east

When, just mounted, Aurora sends forth her streaks

Of amorous potency and blue; and the face of the roost

From which everyone has flown away;

The face of the rushing gopher; the face of the wall

Of the hot, cracking, white clay house in Greece

When the stone hits it; the Russian faucet's face; the face
    of your loved one as depicted on the form

By a "police artist"—she is wanted for entering and
    breaking

The psalmodizing face of the daybreak sea-green palace
    to kidnap the face

Of Egypt, Cleopatra's face, carved by a sculptor

With a face like evening's face—blue, quiet, and stirred
by a breeze; the face of Paris; the beautiful face of
the bean

When it has been smashed; the face of the banana

In its bunch, being thrown into the boat, and while sailing through the air

Thinking, "Someone is going to eat me! but, first, a long,
solemn journey. . . ." A diamond face; the wheel's
face

When it has been going downhill for two hours and suddenly realizes it is no longer a part of its original
wagon—it is now diffuse, or dead, or a "spare part,"
"used," or "free";

The face of the architect who sees his first building crumbling to pieces—he has forgotten to put in the beams!

With a sleepy face—awaking in the morning—"This is
your building!" Moods!

Great Britain's beautiful face during the storm;

William Blake's face; Homer's face; Jack and Jill's faces;
Brenda Starr's insinuating face;

The wind's face as pictured (actually, carved) on the
Tower of the Winds in Athens; the new year's face

When it learns it is our last one on earth; and the domed
face

Of the cemetery plot in which we lie, finally absorbed and
pulled into the other faces;

The face of the burning mouse who lived in the chair

When it was manufactured in Sweden, in someone's
dream; and the gulf's face

When it is full of the Stream; and the egg-like face of the
district manager of "La Lune."

Notice: the eye is a face. Notice: the wave is a fir tree.

Notice: impetuously: the nut's face drank from the
gala's flutes with precarious impunity.
Oh faces like wet summer moods! The face of the cham-
pion on the mountain
When he is straining to pick up a stone; DNA's toothless
face;
The face (I heard this in a story) of the old woman who
had not been down from the mountains since the
nineteenth century
When she was brought down to look at the city—how it
astonished her, showing in her face
And in the movements of her frail body—she wavered
back and forth!
And the sea lion's giant face; the face of the first clouds,
All climbing and responsiveness; the great harvest of the
Meuse's face,
Protectiveness, giant, autumnal, and sunny, suggesting
strong limbs graced by perfect serene contentment;
The Greek face on the jar, so unlimited as to be speechless
captions
Of armor and of sleeping love, the beginnings of face
In the infant or really in the embryo deep in womb valley
Where there is nothing to focus on with face, and the
faces of the happy and satisfied lovers,
One has blonde hair and is a woman, the other has brown
hair and is a man,
They lie on the beach or the bed of contentment mur-
muring "Stone's face"
And "Burnt reed's face" and all the other faces to each
other;
And the breathtaking beauty of the monument-
Al door which the hornets have left unharried, bus face
rushing by, this sandless evening, oh visage, oh where
is that face

Which would have opened these eyes, which, opened,
    might have shown us the truth? the dock's face
When the young boat hits it, it flies apart in merrymaking
    splinters, fond of the boat
And longing for the renewal of its touch; the comic face
Of the drum, when its calfskin is torn during the annual
    concert
To the royal house of Indonesia; and the cook's face
When he has poisoned the wine. I want to take all these
    faces
And make them mine. I want hypodermic
Impossibles, nude Bellini, Popeye inside concrete house,
    with volume
Of bagpipe music concentric, winter, Fra Angelico's face
And the faces he painted, his Virgin, his Musicians; and
    the face
Of the honeybee when it is wet and dripping
With flowery ooze; the face of the feverfew
Which was growing on the mountain until the shears
    sliced it; the face of the beach
Down which twenty people have been running; the face
    in the carpet; the face of the peach
When it was missed by the bullets; faces of a party of
    two
Who have been run over in the mountains;
The grapefruit's face, when the season has been hitting
    it with atmospheric drums;
And the beautiful breasts and eyes and face
Of the woman who was shooting coils (electric ones) off
    the fence at Aleppo, where the shoes of Lord Byron
Were claimed to have been found by a woman with an
    iron face, she had a terrible operation
But her interest in Byron's biography has kept her alive;
    her doctor's face

When he realized the miracle he had performed; Gerard
de Nerval's face, imagined by Soutine
On a summer morning; the club soda factory's face
And the face of its receptionist, yawning, "I am sorry, you
cannot see Sir Abelard Face; he is dead. There are
no more Faces in the world this morning. Goodbye.
The Cavalcade too is closed."
I had so wanted to go with you to the Cavalcade! It was
owned by Sir Abelard Face—
An amusement park ride that took you up into the moun-
tains, as if in a blizzard.
"Goodbye." O seagreen faces! O endless rough loopabouts
of northern and also southern seas!
And faces of larger sea units, royally blue; faces of the
speak-easy
When its boiler room explodes; O scenic faces of the quiet
old women of Peru!
Nose face! illegal face! rocket face! and the face of the
glue
When it is taken to Fiesole and dropped, actually hurled,
down toward Florence
But it doesn't get there and is picked up instead on a dark,
dry route
By a hen with a clucking face, then dropped again
(Because impossible to use it as food) and on the label
of this gluetube the lovely face
Of the Italian model, Angelizia, etched in pink and blue
Against a white cloudy background, she became the mis-
tress
Of the owner of the glue factory, now her face lies bat-
tered
Upon the Tuscan road, but she is happy, the real Angeli-
zia, as she ponders,

Dancing in Tucson, how many times her face is reproduced

And seen around the world; jewelry's faces; faces of firemen; the face of the bowling pin; the rhubarb's face

When it is growing with abandon; the remarkable face of the street, with the people in it, each one speaking, there is such a roar;

The hero of comedy's face, when everything is going well,

And the hippopotamus's face, when he finds he has been put in the wrong zoo, there is no water,

And so he rages, damply, against the summer's bars;

And the chicken's face when the thief has not succeeded in stealing him;

The leader of the orchestra's face when the music flies off as if by magic (the wind is carrying it) and the beautiful valentine face

With gold hair—it is real, you can touch it—reminding me of you;

Alfred Jarry's face on a winter afternoon, when *Ubu Cocu* has just opened at the Théâtre des Champs Elysées

And his followers have mounted him on their shoulders, they wind through the wintry streets with the characteristic abandon

Of open-face sandwiches, and no one is troubled

Except the ocean, whose moon-abiding, satellite face

Speaks to the nuts just once, then speaks no more.

The face of the blue coca-cola when the Acropolis frieze of the Panathenaea has been defaced by secret marbles

Blown from an overhanging hedgehog's pepsi-cola balloon; December's face

When January is over and he again feels the cool form behind him in the parade of months;

The faces of fleas and of firecrackers; the faces of stop-
watches; faces of stock markets, prices going up and
down;
The face of the legs, when you are stepping proudly; and
the face of Alaska;
The faces of hammering fools, faces of elephants; faces of
discarded raincoats; bras' faces; aprons' faces; the
branchings of the yew;
The face of the Unknown Madonna, and the cork's face
At noon, the orange face, the cocoa's face,
The face of the needle, which is chiefly an eye; and the
face of the guru and of the couturier;
The loom's face, when weavers' hands delay; the face of
the crow
When the sky light hits it; and faces with teeth,
Eyes, ears, nose, and cheekbone, faces for cold weather
And steaming faces for hot weather; the face of the owner
of the farm
When the camels have ripped it to pieces; the face on the
fan, I believe it is Herodiade; the stick's face
When it is lying in the garden, and the faces of fliers
When they find that they are floating toward the sun;
The faces of Oz, of China, of Brittany; the face of Chang
Fu and Brit the Chambermaid;
Faces of old Athens and Sparta, faces of Argos, the un-
serious face of Gus the Goose;
Faces of the sunbathers when the clouds split into eight-
een hundred shapes; the amazed face of the mule;
The faces of ants, as they run all around; the face of Lucas
van Leyden; the face of Hindemith; the face of
Childe Harold;
The face of the ox pulling his cart;
The face of Sinbad the Sailor; of Pontius Pilate; of Jesus;
of Nestor;

The faces of Sappho, of Lord Elgin, of Bix Beiderbecke,
of Saint Valentine, of Daphnis and Chloe, of Hero
and Leander;
The face of Hamilcar; the face of Sally Mara; of Sir
Thomas More; of Miss Fujiyama; and of the Duchess
of Falling Out
Of Bed; the face of the earth before it is bitten by the
blue
Of morning; and its daily face afterward;
The faces of fifteen Romantics; the faces of stones;
The face of Haussmann, rebuilding Paris in the eighteen
fifties; the face of Dmitri Mitropoulos; the face of
Mr. Bones; Raymond Queneau's face;
Marcel Raymond's face; the face of the paper on which
the face is drawn of the Queen of Sheba
By an artist with a bearded face—last night he had drunk
a good deal
But today he is happy, to be creating; and the face of the
paper after the drawing is on it
Almost entirely concealing its original face; and the face
of Modern Art
Which is fascinated by this problem; the face of Calvin
Coolidge
And of Gertrude Stein; the underwater tow which brings
all these faces together
And makes them mine, then distends them and scatters
them; the frilly blue lace face of Uncle Ho
And the Winged Victory's face, where it lies, so far lost
beyond all salvation;
And the face of the grass; Alaska's snowy face; the bill-
board face advertising a certain kind of cheese
In Italy; and the fat industrialist's face as he slowly gains
recognition

94

That the heyday of his class is ended; the museum direc-
    tor's face
Who thinks his has come before it has; face of Abelard;
    and face of Peire Vidal; face of the orchid
And of the oyster; the faces of Venice, when everyone is
    wearing a mask—
Some faces! the End; or rather the Beginning; or really
    the End. Faces taking a fall,
Faces to be discriminated, faces in bathtubs, gorgeous,
    risky faces totaling into the billions,
Unimaginable faces shaped like a hat or a football; clowns'
    faces; the face of Saint Ursula
When she was playing a banjo; the face of Einstein; the
    face of the East; the face of grain; the face on the
    weathervane;
The face of Liberal London; the Seine's rusty face; the
    visitor from Mexico, mangled by disease;
Bentham's face; and the face of the secret
Which no one can tell, which is continually bursting from
    these faces—
Noah's face, Kusawara's face, Poussin face, Tiepolo face,
    frog faces, browed faces, angular face, peppy face;
    the faces of seaweed; the faces of seeds.

THE PLEASURES OF PEACE

Another ribald tale of the good times at Madame Lipsky's.
Giorgio Finogle had come in with an imitation of the
latest Russian poet,
The one who wrote the great "Complaint About the Pea-
nut Farm" which I read to you last year at Mrs.
Riley's,
Do you remember? and then of course Giorgio had writ-
ten this imitation
So he came in with it . . . . Where was I and what was I
saying?
The big beer parlor was filled with barmaids and men
named Stuart
Who were all trying to buy a big red pitcher of beer for
an artiste named Alma Stuart
Whom each claimed as his very own because of the simi-
larity in names—
This in essence was Buddy's parody—O Giorgio, you
idiot, Marian Stuart snapped,
It all has something to do with me! But no, Giorgio re-
plied,
Biting in a melancholy way the edge off a cigar-paper-
patterned envelope
In which he had been keeping the Poem for many days
Waiting to show it to his friends. And actually it's not a
parody at all,
I just claimed it was, out of embarrassment. It's a poetic
present for you all,
All of whom I love! Is it capable to love more than one
—I wonder! Alma cried,
And we went out onto the bicycle-shaped dock where a
malicious swarm of mosquitoes

Were parlaying after having invaded the old beer parlor.
The men named Stuart were now involved in a fight to
the death
But the nearer islands lay fair in the white night light.
Shall we embark toward them? I said, placing my hand
upon one exceedingly gentle
And fine. A picture of hairnets is being projected. Here
Comes someone with Alma Stuart! Is it real, this night?
Or have we a gentle fantasy?
The Russian poet appears. He seems to consider it real
all right. He's
Quite angry. Where's the Capitalist fairy that put me
down? he squirts
At our nomadic simplicity. "Complaint About the Pea-
nut Farm" is a terrific poem. Yes,
In a way, yes. The Hairdresser of Night engulfs them all
in foam.

"I love your work, *The Pleasures of Peace*," the Professor
said to me next day;
"I think it adequately encompasses the hysteria of our era
And puts certain people in their rightful place. Chapeau!
Bravo!"
"You don't get it," I said. "I like all this. I called this poem
Pleasures of Peace because I'm not sure they will be last-
ing!
I wanted people to be able to see what these pleasures are
That they may come back to them." "But they are all so
hysterical, so—so transitory,"
The critic replied. "I mean, how can you—what kind of
pleasures are these?
They seem more like pains to me—if I may say what I
mean."
"Well, I don't know, Professor," I said; "permanent joys

Have so far been denied this hysterical person. Though I confess
Far other joys I've had and will describe in time.
And then too there's the pleasure of *writing* these—perhaps to experience is not the same."
The Professor paused, lightly, upon the temple stair.
"I will mention you among the immortals, Ken," he said,
"Because you have the courage of what you believe.
But there I will never mention those sniveling rats
Who only claim to like these things because they're fashionable."
"Professor!" I cried, "My darling! my dream!" And she stripped, and I saw there
Creamy female marble, the waist and thighs of which I had always dreamed.
"Professor! Loved one! why the disguise?" "It was a test," she said,
"Of which you have now only passed the first portion.
You must write More, and More—"
"And be equally persuasive?" I questioned, but She
Had vanished through the Promontory door.

So now I must devote my days to The Pleasures of Peace—
To my contemporaries I'll leave the Horrors of War,
They can do them better than I—each poet shares only a portion
Of the vast Territory of Rhyme. Here in Peace shall I stake out
My temporal and permanent claim. But such silver as I find
I will give to the Universe—the gold I'll put in other poems.
Thus in time there'll be a mountain range of gold

Of considerable interest. Oh may you come back in time
And in my lifetime to see it, most perfect and most de-
lectable reader!
We poets in our youth begin with fantasies,
But then at least we think they may be realities—
The poems we create in our age
Require your hand upon our shoulder, your eye on our
page.

Oh Norman Robinson, the airplane, the village, the bat-
teries,
All this I remember, the Cheese-o-Drome, the phallic
whips, the cucumbers,
The ginger from Australia, the tiny whorehouses no bigger
than a phallus's door,
The evenings without any cucumbers, the phallus's peo-
ple,
The old men trailing blue lassos from door to door,
Who are they all, anyway? I was supposed to be on my
way to Boston
To go to college or get elected to the Legislature
And now I'm here with a lot of cowboys who talk spiritual
Dutch! Let
Me out of here! The lumberyard smelled of the sweet
calla lilies
The courtyard was fragrant with thyme. I released your
hand
And walked into the Mexicana Valley, where my father
was first a cowboy.
I take a genuine interest in the people of this country
Yes sir I think you might even call me Coleman the Dutch
but now the night sky fills with fairies
It is all that modern stuff beginning to happen again,
well, let it—

We robots tell the truth about old Gabby
But when the shirtfront scuffs we yell for Labby
It is a scientific stunt
Which Moonlight has brought you from Australia
Sit it down on this chair shaped like a pirate
When you have come three times I will give you a silver-
    ware hazelnut
With which you can escape from time
For this I'm calling in all the poets who take dope
To help me out, here they come
Oh is there room in the universe for such as we?
They say, but though we cannot make our Time
Stand still, yet we'll him silver like a Dime.
Inversions yet! and not even sexual ones!
O Labrador, you are the sexual Pennsylvania of our times!

Chapter Thirty Seven.
On the Planisphere everyone was having a nut
When suddenly my Lulu appeared.
She was a big broad about six feet seven
And she had a red stone in her ear
Which was stringent in its beauty.
I demanded at once the removal of people from the lobby
So we could begin to down ABC tablets and start to feel
    funny
But Mordecai La Schlomp our Leader replied that we did
    not need any
That a person could feel good without any artificial means.

If I love you, a mother bird says to the whalebird's father,
It's not because I want you to be untrue to Mrs. Senior
    Whalebird, now you really know that don't you?
You—treacherous bitch! shouted the enraged Whalebird
    leaping onto her painted nylon pajamas

100

With his oriental feet until she screamed and bejibbered
And the cast-filled eye of the moon sinks into the sea
Sometimes wandering along this coast a lonely Indian
    boy
Would begin to cry for his mamma, and a wandering star
Would spurt in sympathy
Some silver come into the shiny sea.

Good night, Frank Robinson
And Gypsy Rose Lee,
I am tired and I want to lie down.
All day I have walked along this deliberate coastline
Trying as hard as I could to write everything down—
And now you see what has come of it, I mean one star,
I mean one star and all that is left in the cupboard
Is one violet couplet of lights.
Perhaps if you could agree
To step out of that coat. . . .

Here are listed all the Pleasures of Peace that there could
    possibly be.
Among them are the pleasures of Memory (which Del-
    more Schwartz celebrated), the pleasures of auton-
    omy,
The pleasures of agoraphobia and the sudden release
Of the agoraphobic person from the identified market-
    place, the pleasures of roving over you
And rolling over the beach, of being in a complicated car,
    of sleeping,
Of drawing ropes with you, of planning a deranged comic
    strip, of shifting knees
At the accelerator pump, of blasphemy, of cobra settle-
    ment in a dilapidated skin country

Without clops, and therefore every pleasure is also in-
cluded; which, after these—

Oh the Pleasures of Peace are infinite and they cannot be
counted—
One single piece of pink mint chewing gum contains more
pleasures
Than the whole rude gallery of war! And the moon passes
by
In an otherwise undistinguished lesson on the geography
of this age
Which has had fifty-seven good lovers and ninety-six
wars. By Giorgio Finogle.

It turns out that we're competing for the Peace Award,
Giorgio Finogle and I. We go into the hair parlor, the
barber—
We get to talking about war and about peace.
The barber feels that we are really good people at heart
Even though his own views turn out to be conservative.
"I've read Finogle's piece, the part of it that was in
Smut," he
Says, "and I liked it. Yours, Koch, I haven't yet seen,
But Alyne and Francie told me that you were the better
poet."
"I don't know," I said. "Giorgio is pretty good." And
Giorgio comes back from the bathroom
Now, with a grin on his face. "I've got an idea for my
Pleasures of Peace," he says; "I'm going to make it include
Each person in the universe discussing their own bag—
Translation, their main interest, and what they want
to be—"
"You'll never finish it, Giorgio," I said. "At least I'll
Get started," he replied, and he ran out of the barbershop.

In the quiet night we take turns riding horseback and
falling asleep.
Your breasts are more beautiful than a gold mine.
I think I'll become a professional man.
The reason we are up-to-date is we're some kind of freaks.
I don't know what to tell the old man
But he is concerned with two kinds of phenomena and I
am interested in neither. What *are* you interested in?
Being some kind of freaks, I think. Let's go to Transyl-
vania.
I don't understand your buddy all the time. Who?
The one with HANDLEBAR written across his head.
He's a good guy, he just doesn't see the difference be-
tween a man and a bike. If I love you
It's because you belong to and have a sublime tolerance
For such people. Yes, but in later life, I mean—
It is Present Life we've got to keep up on the screen,
Isn't it. Well yes, she said, but—
I am very happy that you are interested in it. The French
poodle stopped being Irish entirely
And we are all out of the other breeds.
The society woman paused, daintily, upon the hotel stair.
No, I must have a poodle, said she; not an Irish setter
Would satisfy me in my mad passion for the poodle
breeds!
As usual, returning to the bed
I find that you are inside it and sound asleep. I smile
happily and look at your head.
It is regular-size and has beautiful blonde hair all around
it.
Some is lying across the pillow. I touch it with my feet
Then leap out the window into the public square,
And I tune my guitar.

"O Mistress Mine, where are you roving?" That's my tune!
   roars Finogle, and he
Comes raging out of the *Beefsteak*—I was going to put
   that in MY Pleasures of Peace.
Oh normal comportment! even you too I shall include in
   the Pleasures of Peace,
And you, relative humidity five hundred and sixty-two
   degrees!
But what of you, poor sad glorious aqueduct
Of boorish ashes made by cigarettes smoked at the Cup-
   cake
Award—And Sue Ellen Musgrove steps on one of my feet.
   "Hello!"
She says. "You're that famous COKE, aren't you,
That no one can drink? When are you going to give us
   your famous Iliad
That everyone's been talking of, I mean your Pleasures of
   Peace!"

Life changes as the universe changes, but the universe
   changes
More slowly, as bedevilments increase.
Sunlight comes through a clot for example
Which Zoo Man has thrown on the floor. It is the Night
   of the Painted Pajamas
And the Liberals are weeping for peace. The Conserva-
   tives are raging for it.
The Independents are staging a parade. And we are com-
   pletely naked
Walking through the bedroom for peace. I have this
   friend who had myopia
So he always had to get very close to people
And girls thought he was trying to make out—

Why didn't he get glasses?—He was a Pacifist! The Moon
   shall overcome!

Outside in the bar yard the Grecians are screaming for
   peace
And the Alsatians, the Albanians, the Alesians, the Ru-
   bans, the Aleutians,
And the slanty-eyed Iranians, all, all are screaming for
   peace.
They shall win it, their peace, because I am going to help
   them!
And he leaped out the window for peace!
Headline: GIORGIO FINOGLE,
NOTED POET, LAST NIGHT LEAPED OUT THE
   WINDOW FOR PEACE.
ASIDE FROM HEAD INJURIES HIS CONDITION IS
   REPORTED NORMAL.
But Giorgio never was normal! Oh the horrors of peace,
I mean of peace-fighting! But Giorgio is all right,
He is still completely himself. "I am going to throw this
   hospital
Bed out the window for peace," when we see him, he says.
And, "Well, I guess your poem will be getting way ahead
   of mine now," he says
Sadly, ripping up an envelope for peace and weakly hold-
   ing out his hand
For my girl, Ellen, to stroke it; "I will no longer be the
   most famous poet
For peace. You will, and you know it." "But you jumped
   out the
Window, Finogle," I said, "and your deed shall live longer
In men's imaginations than any verse." But he looked at
   the sky

105

Through the window's beautiful eye and he said, "Kenneth, I have not written one word
Of my Poem for Peace for three weeks. I've struck a snarl
And that's why (I believe) I jumped out the
Window—pure poetic frustration. Now tell them all that, how
They'll despise me, oh sob sob—" "Giorgio," I said, trying to calm him down but laughing
So hard I could barely digest the dinner of imagination
In which your breasts were featured as on a Popeye card
When winter has lighted the lanterns and the falls are asleep
Waiting for next day's shards, "Giorgio," I said, "the pleasures—"
But hysteria transported us all.

When I awoke you were in a star-shaped muffin, I was in a loaf of bread
Shaped like a camera, and Giorgio was still in his hospital bed
But a huge baker loomed over us. One false moof and I die you! he said
In a murderous throaty voice and I believe in the yellow leaves, the
Orange, the red leaves of autumn, the tan leaves, and the promoted ones
Of green, of green and blue. Sometimes walking through an ordinary garden
You will see a bird, and the overcoat will fall from your
Shoulders, slightly, exposing one beautiful curve
On which sunbeams alighting forget to speak a single word
To their parent sun and are thus cut off

Without a heating unit, but need none being on your
    breast
Which I have re-christened "Loaves" for the beginning of
    this year
In which I hope the guns won't fire any more, the baker
    sang
To his baker lady, and then he had totally disappeared.
It looks as though everyone were going to be on our
    side!

And the flowers came out, and they were on our side,
Even the yellow little ones that grow beside your door
And the huge orange ones were bending to one side
As we walked past them, I looked into your blue eyes
And I said, "If we come out of this door
Any more, let it be to enter only this nervous paradise
Of peaceful living conditions, and if Giorgio is roped down
Let them untie him, so he can throw his hospital bed out
    the door
For all we need besides peace, which is considerable, but
    first we need that—"

Daredevil, Julian and Maddalo, and John L. Lewis
Are running down the stairways for peace, they are gath-
    ering the ice
And throwing it in buckets, they are raising purple para-
    sols for peace
And on top of these old sunlight sings her song, "New
    lights, old lights again, blue lights for peace,
Red lights for the low, insulted parasol, and a few crutches
    thrown around for peace"—
Oh contentment is the key
To continuing exploration of the nations and their feet;

Therefore, andiamo—the footfall is waiting in the car
And peaceful are the markets and the sneaks;
Peaceful are the Garfinkle ping-pong balls
And peaceful are the blooms beneath the sea
Peaceful are the unreserved airplane loops and the popu-
    larly guided blips
Also the Robert Herrick stone sings a peaceful song
And the banana factory is getting hip, and the pigs' Easter
    party too is beginning to join in a general celebration
And the women and men of old Peru and young Haifa
    and ancient Japan and beautiful young rippling Lake
    Tahoe
And hairy old Boston and young Freeport and young
    Santo Domingo and old father Candelabra the Chief-
    tain of Hoboes
Are rolling around the parapets for peace, and now the
    matadors are throwing in
Huge blops of canvas and the postgraduates are filling in
As grocery dates at peanut dances and the sunlight is
    filling in
Every human world canvas with huge and luminous
    pleasure gobs of peace—
And the Tintorettos are looking very purple for peace
And the oyster campus is beginning its peaceful song—

Oh let it be concluded, including the medals!
Peace will come thrusting out of the sky
Tomorrow morning, to bomb us into quietude.
For a while we can bid goodbye
To the frenesies of this poem, The Pleasures of Peace.
When there is peace we will not need anything but bread
Stars and plaster with which to begin.
Roaming from one beard to another we shall take the tin
From the mines and give it to roaring Fidel Castro.

Where Mao Tse Tung lies buried in ocean fields of sleep-
     ing cars
Our Lorcaesque decisions will clonk him out
And resurrect him to the rosebuddy sky
Of early evening. And the whip-shaped generals of Hanoi
Shall be taken in overcoats to visit the sky
And the earth will be gasping for joy!

"A wonder!" "A rout!" "No need now for any further
     poems!" "A Banzai for peace!" "He can speak to us
     all!"
And "Great, man!" "Impressive!" "Something new for you,
     Ken!" "Astounding!" "A real
Epic!" "The worst poem I have ever read!" "Abominably
     tasteless!" "Too funny!" "Dead, man!
A cop out! a real white man's poem! a folderol of honkie
     blank spitzenburger smugglerout Caucasian gyp
Of phony bourgeois peace poetry, a total shrig!" "Terrific!"
     "I will expect you at six!"
"A lovely starry catalogue for peace!" "Is it Shakespeare
     or Byron who breathes
In the lines of his poem?" "You have given us the Plea-
     sures of Peace,
Now where is the real thing?" "Koch has studied his his-
     tory!" "Bold!" "Stunning!" "It touches us like leaves
Sparkling in April—but is that all there is
To his peace plea?" Well, you be the one
To conclude it, if you think it needs more—I want to end
     it,
I want to see real Peace again! Oh peace bams!
I need your assistance—and peace drams, distilling
     through the world! peace lamps, be shining! and
     peace lambs, rumble up the shore!

O Goddess, sweet Muse, I'm stopping—now show us
where you are!

And the big boats come sailing into the harbor for peace
And the little apes are running around the jungle for
peace
And the day (that is, the star of day, the sun) is shining
for peace
Somewhere a moustachioed student is puzzling over the
works of Raymond Roussel for peace
And the Mediterranean peach trees are fast asleep for
peace
With their pink arms akimbo and the blue plums of
Switzerland for peace
And the monkeys are climbing for coconuts and peace
The Hawaiian palm
And serpents are writhing for peace—those are snakes—
And the Alps, Mount Vesuvius, all the really big impor-
tant mountains
Are rising for peace, and they're filled with rocks—surely
it won't be long;
And Leonardo da Vinci's *Last Supper* is moving across the
monastery wall
A few micrometers for peace, and Paolo Uccello's red
horses
Are turning a little redder for peace, and the Anglo-Saxon
dining hall
Begins glowing like crazy, and Beowulf, Robert E. Lee,
Sir Barbarossa, and Baron Jeep
Are sleeping on the railways for peace and darting around
the harbor
And leaping into the sailboats and the sailboats will go on
And underneath the sailboats the sea will go on and we
will go on

And the birds will go on and the snappy words will go on
And the tea sky and the sloped marine sky
And the hustle of beans will go on and the unserious canoe
It will all be going on in connection with you, peace, and
    my poem, like a Cadillac of wampum
Unredeemed and flying madly, will go exploding through
New cities sweet inflated, planispheres, ingenious hair, a
    camera smashing
Badinage, cerebral stands of atmospheres, unequaled,
    dreamed of
Empeacements, candled piers, fumisteries, emphatic
    moods, terrestialism's
Crackle, love's flat, sun's sweets, oh peace, to you.